The Easiest Way to Keep Track of Your Day: WEEKLY POCKET PLANNER BOOK

Activinotes

DAILY JOURNALS, PLANNERS, NOTEBOOKS AND OTHER BLANK BOOKS

_____

Name

_____

Address

_____

Contact Address

_____

Email Address

MY WEEK

MONTH

WEEK

MONDAY

....

....

....

....

....

TUESDAY

....

....

....

....

....

WEDNESDAY

....

....

....

....

....

THURSDAY

....

....

....

....

....

FRIDAY

....

....

....

....

....

THIS WEEKEND

....

....

....

....

....

WEEKLY GOALS

_____ ▢

_____ ▢

_____ ▢

_____ ▢

_____ ▢

_____ ▢

_____ ▢

_____ ▢

_____ ▢

_____ ▢

NOTES

_____

_____

_____

THIS WEEK'S

DATES

PRIORITIES

TO DO

- [ ] _____
- [ ] _____
- [ ] _____
- [ ] _____
- [ ] _____

- [ ] _____
- [ ] _____
- [ ] _____
- [ ] _____
- [ ] _____

MY WEEK

MONTH

WEEK

MONDAY

....

....

....

....

....

TUESDAY

....

....

....

....

....

WEDNESDAY

....

....

....

....

....

THURSDAY

....

....

....

....

....

FRIDAY

· ·

· ·

· ·

· ·

· ·

THIS WEEKEND

· ·

· ·

· ·

· ·

· ·

WEEKLY GOALS

_____

_____

_____

_____

_____

_____

_____

_____

_____

_____

NOTES

_____

_____

_____

THIS WEEK'S

DATES

PRIORITIES

TO DO

- ☐ _____
- ☐ _____
- ☐ _____
- ☐ _____
- ☐ _____

- ☐ _____
- ☐ _____
- ☐ _____
- ☐ _____
- ☐ _____

MY WEEK

MONTH

WEEK

MONDAY

....
....
....
....
....

TUESDAY

....
....
....
....
....

WEDNESDAY

....
....
....
....
....

THURSDAY

....
....
....
....
....

FRIDAY

....

....

....

....

....

THIS WEEKEND

....

....

....

....

....

WEEKLY GOALS

_____ ▢

_____ ▢

_____ ▢

_____ ▢

_____ ▢

_____ ▢

_____ ▢

_____ ▢

_____ ▢

_____ ▢

NOTES

_____

_____

_____

THIS WEEK'S

DATES

PRIORITIES

TO DO

- [ ] _____
- [ ] _____
- [ ] _____
- [ ] _____
- [ ] _____

- [ ] _____
- [ ] _____
- [ ] _____
- [ ] _____
- [ ] _____

MY WEEK

MONTH

WEEK

MONDAY

....
....
....
....
....

TUESDAY

....
....
....
....
....

WEDNESDAY

....
....
....
....
....

THURSDAY

....
....
....
....
....

FRIDAY

· ·

· ·

· ·

· ·

· ·

THIS WEEKEND

· ·

· ·

· ·

· ·

· ·

WEEKLY GOALS

NOTES

THIS WEEK'S

DATES

PRIORITIES

TO DO

- ☐ _____
- ☐ _____
- ☐ _____
- ☐ _____
- ☐ _____

- ☐ _____
- ☐ _____
- ☐ _____
- ☐ _____
- ☐ _____

MY WEEK

MONDAY

....

....

....

....

....

TUESDAY

....

....

....

....

WEDNESDAY

....

....

....

....

....

THURSDAY

....

....

....

....

....

FRIDAY

....

....

....

....

....

THIS WEEKEND

....

....

....

....

....

WEEKLY GOALS

_____ ▪

_____ ▪

_____ ▪

_____ ▪

_____ ▪

_____ ▪

_____ ▪

_____ ▪

_____ ▪

_____ ▪

NOTES

_____

_____

_____

THIS WEEK'S

DATES

PRIORITIES

TO DO

- ☐ _____
- ☐ _____
- ☐ _____
- ☐ _____
- ☐ _____

- ☐ _____
- ☐ _____
- ☐ _____
- ☐ _____
- ☐ _____

MY WEEK

MONTH

WEEK

MONDAY

··
··
··
··
··

TUESDAY

··
··
··
··
··

WEDNESDAY

··
··
··
··
··

THURSDAY

··
··
··
··
··

FRIDAY

....

....

....

....

....

THIS WEEKEND

....

....

....

....

....

WEEKLY GOALS

_____ ▢

_____ ▢

_____ ▢

_____ ▢

_____ ▢

_____ ▢

_____ ▢

_____ ▢

_____ ▢

_____ ▢

NOTES

_____

_____

_____

THIS WEEK'S

DATES

PRIORITIES

TO DO

- [ ] _____
- [ ] _____
- [ ] _____
- [ ] _____
- [ ] _____

- [ ] _____
- [ ] _____
- [ ] _____
- [ ] _____
- [ ] _____

MY WEEK

MONTH

WEEK

MONDAY

....
....
....
....
....

TUESDAY

....
....
....
....
....

WEDNESDAY

....
....
....
....
....

THURSDAY

....
....
....
....
....

FRIDAY

....

....

....

....

....

THIS WEEKEND

....

....

....

....

....

WEEKLY GOALS

_____ ☐

_____ ☐

_____ ☐

_____ ☐

_____ ☐

_____ ☐

_____ ☐

_____ ☐

_____ ☐

_____ ☐

NOTES

_____

_____

_____

THIS WEEK'S

DATES

PRIORITIES

TO DO

- [ ] _____
- [ ] _____
- [ ] _____
- [ ] _____
- [ ] _____

- [ ] _____
- [ ] _____
- [ ] _____
- [ ] _____
- [ ] _____

MY WEEK

MONTH

WEEK

MONDAY

....
....
....
....
....

TUESDAY

....
....
....
....
....

WEDNESDAY

....
....
....
....
....

THURSDAY

....
....
....
....
....

FRIDAY

....

....

....

....

....

THIS WEEKEND

....

....

....

....

....

WEEKLY GOALS

_____ ▢

_____ ▢

_____ ▢

_____ ▢

_____ ▢

_____ ▢

_____ ▢

_____ ▢

_____ ▢

_____ ▢

NOTES

_____

_____

_____

THIS WEEK'S

DATES

PRIORITIES

TO DO

- [ ] _____
- [ ] _____
- [ ] _____
- [ ] _____
- [ ] _____

- [ ] _____
- [ ] _____
- [ ] _____
- [ ] _____
- [ ] _____

MY WEEK

MONTH

WEEK

MONDAY

....
....
....
....
....

TUESDAY

....
....
....
....
....

WEDNESDAY

....
....
....
....
....

THURSDAY

....
....
....
....
....

FRIDAY

....

....

....

....

....

THIS WEEKEND

....

....

....

....

....

WEEKLY GOALS

_____ ☐

_____ ☐

_____ ☐

_____ ☐

_____ ☐

_____ ☐

_____ ☐

_____ ☐

_____ ☐

_____ ☐

NOTES

_____

_____

_____

THIS WEEK'S

DATES

PRIORITIES

TO DO

- [ ] _____
- [ ] _____
- [ ] _____
- [ ] _____
- [ ] _____

- [ ] _____
- [ ] _____
- [ ] _____
- [ ] _____
- [ ] _____

FRIDAY

....

....

....

....

....

THIS WEEKEND

....

....

....

....

....

WEEKLY GOALS

_____ ▢

_____ ▢

_____ ▢

_____ ▢

_____ ▢

_____ ▢

_____ ▢

_____ ▢

_____ ▢

_____ ▢

NOTES

_____

_____

_____

THIS WEEK'S

DATES

PRIORITIES

TO DO

☐ _____   ☐ _____

☐ _____   ☐ _____

☐ _____   ☐ _____

☐ _____   ☐ _____

☐ _____   ☐ _____

MY WEEK

MONTH

WEEK

MONDAY

·····················
·····················
·····················
·····················
·····················

TUESDAY

·····················
·····················
·····················
·····················
·····················

WEDNESDAY

·····················
·····················
·····················
·····················
·····················

THURSDAY

·····················
·····················
·····················
·····················
·····················

FRIDAY

....

....

....

....

....

THIS WEEKEND

....

....

....

....

....

WEEKLY GOALS

_____ ▢   _____ ▢

_____ ▢   _____ ▢

_____ ▢   _____ ▢

_____ ▢   _____ ▢

_____ ▢   _____ ▢

NOTES

_____

_____

_____

THIS WEEK'S

DATES

PRIORITIES

TO DO

- ☐ _____
- ☐ _____
- ☐ _____
- ☐ _____
- ☐ _____

- ☐ _____
- ☐ _____
- ☐ _____
- ☐ _____
- ☐ _____

MY WEEK

MONDAY

....
....
....
....
....

TUESDAY

....
....
....
....

WEDNESDAY

....
....
....
....

THURSDAY

....
....
....
....
....

FRIDAY

....

....

....

....

....

THIS WEEKEND

....

....

....

....

....

WEEKLY GOALS

_____ ☐		_____ ☐
_____ ☐		_____ ☐
_____ ☐		_____ ☐
_____ ☐		_____ ☐
_____ ☐		_____ ☐

NOTES

_____

_____

_____

THIS WEEK'S

DATES

PRIORITIES

TO DO

- ☐ _____
- ☐ _____
- ☐ _____
- ☐ _____
- ☐ _____

- ☐ _____
- ☐ _____
- ☐ _____
- ☐ _____
- ☐ _____

MY WEEK

MONTH

WEEK

MONDAY

....
....
....
....
....

TUESDAY

....
....
....
....
....

WEDNESDAY

....
....
....
....
....

THURSDAY

....
....
....
....
....

FRIDAY

....

....

....

....

....

THIS WEEKEND

....

....

....

....

....

WEEKLY GOALS

_____ ▪

_____ ▪

_____ ▪

_____ ▪

_____ ▪

_____ ▪

_____ ▪

_____ ▪

_____ ▪

_____ ▪

NOTES

_____

_____

_____

THIS WEEK'S

DATES

PRIORITIES

TO DO

- ☐ _____
- ☐ _____
- ☐ _____
- ☐ _____
- ☐ _____

- ☐ _____
- ☐ _____
- ☐ _____
- ☐ _____
- ☐ _____

MY WEEK

MONTH

WEEK

MONDAY

....
....
....
....
....

TUESDAY

....
....
....
....

WEDNESDAY

....
....
....
....

THURSDAY

....
....
....
....
....

FRIDAY

....
....
....
....
....

THIS WEEKEND

....
....
....
....
....

WEEKLY GOALS

_____ ☐
_____ ☐
_____ ☐
_____ ☐
_____ ☐

_____ ☐
_____ ☐
_____ ☐
_____ ☐
_____ ☐

NOTES

_____

_____

_____

THIS WEEK'S

DATES

PRIORITIES

TO DO

- [ ] _____
- [ ] _____
- [ ] _____
- [ ] _____
- [ ] _____

- [ ] _____
- [ ] _____
- [ ] _____
- [ ] _____
- [ ] _____

MY WEEK

MONTH

WEEK

MONDAY

....

....

....

....

....

TUESDAY

....

....

....

....

....

WEDNESDAY

....

....

....

....

....

THURSDAY

....

....

....

....

....

FRIDAY

....

....

....

....

....

THIS WEEKEND

....

....

....

....

....

WEEKLY GOALS

_____ ☐   _____ ☐

_____ ☐   _____ ☐

_____ ☐   _____ ☐

_____ ☐   _____ ☐

_____ ☐   _____ ☐

NOTES

_____

_____

_____

THIS WEEK'S

DATES

PRIORITIES

TO DO

- [ ] _____
- [ ] _____
- [ ] _____
- [ ] _____
- [ ] _____

- [ ] _____
- [ ] _____
- [ ] _____
- [ ] _____
- [ ] _____

MY WEEK

MONDAY

....

....

....

....

....

TUESDAY

....

....

....

....

....

WEDNESDAY

....

....

....

....

....

THURSDAY

....

....

....

....

....

FRIDAY

....

....

....

....

....

THIS WEEKEND

....

....

....

....

....

WEEKLY GOALS

_____ ☐

_____ ☐

_____ ☐

_____ ☐

_____ ☐

_____ ☐

_____ ☐

_____ ☐

_____ ☐

_____ ☐

NOTES

_____

_____

_____

THIS WEEK'S

DATES

PRIORITIES

TO DO

- [ ] _____
- [ ] _____
- [ ] _____
- [ ] _____
- [ ] _____

- [ ] _____
- [ ] _____
- [ ] _____
- [ ] _____
- [ ] _____

MY WEEK

MONTH

WEEK

MONDAY

....
....
....
....
....

TUESDAY

....
....
....
....
....

WEDNESDAY

....
....
....
....
....

THURSDAY

....
....
....
....
....

FRIDAY

....

....

....

....

....

THIS WEEKEND

....

....

....

....

....

WEEKLY GOALS

_____ ⬜

_____ ⬜

_____ ⬜

_____ ⬜

_____ ⬜

_____ ⬜

_____ ⬜

_____ ⬜

_____ ⬜

_____ ⬜

NOTES

_____

_____

_____

THIS WEEK'S

DATES

PRIORITIES

TO DO

- ☐ _____
- ☐ _____
- ☐ _____
- ☐ _____
- ☐ _____

- ☐ _____
- ☐ _____
- ☐ _____
- ☐ _____
- ☐ _____

MY WEEK

MONTH

WEEK

MONDAY

....

....

....

....

....

TUESDAY

....

....

....

....

....

WEDNESDAY

....

....

....

....

....

THURSDAY

....

....

....

....

....

FRIDAY

....

....

....

....

....

THIS WEEKEND

....

....

....

....

....

WEEKLY GOALS

_____ ☐

_____ ☐

_____ ☐

_____ ☐

_____ ☐

_____ ☐

_____ ☐

_____ ☐

_____ ☐

_____ ☐

NOTES

_____

_____

_____

THIS WEEK'S

DATES

PRIORITIES

TO DO

- [ ] _____
- [ ] _____
- [ ] _____
- [ ] _____
- [ ] _____

- [ ] _____
- [ ] _____
- [ ] _____
- [ ] _____
- [ ] _____

MY WEEK

MONTH

WEEK

MONDAY

....

....

....

....

....

TUESDAY

....

....

....

....

....

WEDNESDAY

....

....

....

....

....

THURSDAY

....

....

....

....

....

FRIDAY

....

....

....

....

....

THIS WEEKEND

....

....

....

....

....

WEEKLY GOALS

_____ ☐

_____ ☐

_____ ☐

_____ ☐

_____ ☐

_____ ☐

_____ ☐

_____ ☐

_____ ☐

_____ ☐

NOTES

_____

_____

_____

THIS WEEK'S

DATES

PRIORITIES

TO DO

- ☐ _____
- ☐ _____
- ☐ _____
- ☐ _____
- ☐ _____

- ☐ _____
- ☐ _____
- ☐ _____
- ☐ _____
- ☐ _____

MY WEEK

MONTH

WEEK

MONDAY

....

....

....

....

....

TUESDAY

....

....

....

....

....

WEDNESDAY

....

....

....

....

....

THURSDAY

....

....

....

....

....

FRIDAY

....

....

....

....

....

THIS WEEKEND

....

....

....

....

....

WEEKLY GOALS

_____ ☐

_____ ☐

_____ ☐

_____ ☐

_____ ☐

_____ ☐

_____ ☐

_____ ☐

_____ ☐

_____ ☐

NOTES

_____

_____

_____

THIS WEEK'S

DATES

PRIORITIES

TO DO

- ☐ _____
- ☐ _____
- ☐ _____
- ☐ _____
- ☐ _____

- ☐ _____
- ☐ _____
- ☐ _____
- ☐ _____
- ☐ _____

MY WEEK

MONTH

WEEK

MONDAY

....

....

....

....

....

TUESDAY

....

....

....

....

....

WEDNESDAY

....

....

....

....

....

THURSDAY

....

....

....

....

FRIDAY

....

....

....

....

....

THIS WEEKEND

....

....

....

....

....

WEEKLY GOALS

_____ ▪

_____ ▪

_____ ▪

_____ ▪

_____ ▪

_____ ▪

_____ ▪

_____ ▪

_____ ▪

_____ ▪

NOTES

_____

_____

_____

THIS WEEK'S

DATES

PRIORITIES

TO DO

- ☐ _____
- ☐ _____
- ☐ _____
- ☐ _____
- ☐ _____

- ☐ _____
- ☐ _____
- ☐ _____
- ☐ _____
- ☐ _____

MY WEEK

MONTH

WEEK

MONDAY

....
....
....
....
....

TUESDAY

....
....
....
....
....

WEDNESDAY

....
....
....
....
....

THURSDAY

....
....
....
....
....

FRIDAY

....

....

....

....

....

THIS WEEKEND

....

....

....

....

....

WEEKLY GOALS

_____ ▪

_____ ▪

_____ ▪

_____ ▪

_____ ▪

_____ ▪

_____ ▪

_____ ▪

_____ ▪

_____ ▪

NOTES

_____

_____

_____

THIS WEEK'S

DATES

PRIORITIES

TO DO

- ☐ _____
- ☐ _____
- ☐ _____
- ☐ _____
- ☐ _____

- ☐ _____
- ☐ _____
- ☐ _____
- ☐ _____
- ☐ _____

MY WEEK

MONTH

WEEK

MONDAY

....
....
....
....
....

TUESDAY

....
....
....
....
....

WEDNESDAY

....
....
....
....
....

THURSDAY

....
....
....
....
....

FRIDAY

....

....

....

....

....

THIS WEEKEND

....

....

....

....

....

WEEKLY GOALS

_____ ▢

_____ ▢

_____ ▢

_____ ▢

_____ ▢

_____ ▢

_____ ▢

_____ ▢

_____ ▢

_____ ▢

NOTES

_____

_____

_____

THIS WEEK'S

DATES

PRIORITIES

TO DO

- ☐ _____
- ☐ _____
- ☐ _____
- ☐ _____
- ☐ _____

- ☐ _____
- ☐ _____
- ☐ _____
- ☐ _____
- ☐ _____

MY WEEK

MONTH

WEEK

MONDAY

....
....
....
....
....

TUESDAY

....
....
....
....
....

WEDNESDAY

....
....
....
....

THURSDAY

....
....
....
....

FRIDAY

....

....

....

....

....

THIS WEEKEND

....

....

....

....

....

WEEKLY GOALS

_____ ☐

_____ ☐

_____ ☐

_____ ☐

_____ ☐

_____ ☐

_____ ☐

_____ ☐

_____ ☐

_____ ☐

NOTES

_____

_____

_____

THIS WEEK'S

DATES

PRIORITIES

TO DO

- [ ] _____
- [ ] _____
- [ ] _____
- [ ] _____
- [ ] _____

- [ ] _____
- [ ] _____
- [ ] _____
- [ ] _____
- [ ] _____

MY WEEK

MONDAY

....
....
....
....
....

TUESDAY

....
....
....
....
....

WEDNESDAY

....
....
....
....
....

THURSDAY

....
....
....
....
....

FRIDAY

· ·

· ·

· ·

· ·

· ·

THIS WEEKEND

· ·

· ·

· ·

· ·

· ·

WEEKLY GOALS

_____

_____

_____

_____

_____

_____

_____

_____

_____

_____

NOTES

_____

_____

_____

THIS WEEK'S

DATES

PRIORITIES

TO DO

- ☐ _____
- ☐ _____
- ☐ _____
- ☐ _____
- ☐ _____

- ☐ _____
- ☐ _____
- ☐ _____
- ☐ _____
- ☐ _____

MY WEEK

MONTH

WEEK

MONDAY

·····················
·····················
·····················
·····················
·····················

TUESDAY

·····················
·····················
·····················
·····················
·····················

WEDNESDAY

·····················
·····················
·····················
·····················
·····················

THURSDAY

·····················
·····················
·····················
·····················
·····················

FRIDAY

....

....

....

....

....

THIS WEEKEND

....

....

....

....

....

WEEKLY GOALS

_____ □

_____ □

_____ □

_____ □

_____ □

_____ □

_____ □

_____ □

_____ □

_____ □

NOTES

_____

_____

_____

THIS WEEK'S

DATES

PRIORITIES

TO DO

- ☐ _____
- ☐ _____
- ☐ _____
- ☐ _____
- ☐ _____

- ☐ _____
- ☐ _____
- ☐ _____
- ☐ _____
- ☐ _____

MY WEEK

MONTH

WEEK

MONDAY

....
....
....
....
....

TUESDAY

....
....
....
....
....

WEDNESDAY

....
....
....
....
....

THURSDAY

....
....
....
....
....

FRIDAY

....

....

....

....

....

THIS WEEKEND

....

....

....

....

....

WEEKLY GOALS

_____ ▢

_____ ▢

_____ ▢

_____ ▢

_____ ▢

_____ ▢

_____ ▢

_____ ▢

_____ ▢

_____ ▢

NOTES

_____

_____

_____

THIS WEEK'S

DATES

PRIORITIES

TO DO

- ☐ _____
- ☐ _____
- ☐ _____
- ☐ _____
- ☐ _____

- ☐ _____
- ☐ _____
- ☐ _____
- ☐ _____
- ☐ _____

MY WEEK

MONTH

WEEK

MONDAY

....
....
....
....
....

TUESDAY

....
....
....
....
....

WEDNESDAY

....
....
....
....
....

THURSDAY

....
....
....
....
....

FRIDAY

....

....

....

....

....

THIS WEEKEND

....

....

....

....

....

WEEKLY GOALS

_____ ☐

_____ ☐

_____ ☐

_____ ☐

_____ ☐

_____ ☐

_____ ☐

_____ ☐

_____ ☐

_____ ☐

NOTES

_____

_____

_____

THIS WEEK'S

DATES

PRIORITIES

TO DO

- [ ] _____
- [ ] _____
- [ ] _____
- [ ] _____
- [ ] _____

- [ ] _____
- [ ] _____
- [ ] _____
- [ ] _____
- [ ] _____

MY WEEK

MONTH

WEEK

MONDAY

....

....

....

....

....

TUESDAY

....

....

....

....

....

WEDNESDAY

....

....

....

....

....

THURSDAY

....

....

....

....

....

FRIDAY

....

....

....

....

....

THIS WEEKEND

....

....

....

....

....

WEEKLY GOALS

_____ ▢

_____ ▢

_____ ▢

_____ ▢

_____ ▢

_____ ▢

_____ ▢

_____ ▢

_____ ▢

_____ ▢

NOTES

_____

_____

_____

THIS WEEK'S

DATES

PRIORITIES

TO DO

- ☐ _____
- ☐ _____
- ☐ _____
- ☐ _____
- ☐ _____

- ☐ _____
- ☐ _____
- ☐ _____
- ☐ _____
- ☐ _____

MY WEEK

MONTH

WEEK

MONDAY

·····················
·····················
·····················
·····················
·····················

TUESDAY

·····················
·····················
·····················
·····················

WEDNESDAY

·····················
·····················
·····················
·····················
·····················

THURSDAY

·····················
·····················
·····················
·····················

FRIDAY

....

....

....

....

....

THIS WEEKEND

....

....

....

....

....

WEEKLY GOALS

_____ ▪

_____ ▪

_____ ▪

_____ ▪

_____ ▪

_____ ▪

_____ ▪

_____ ▪

_____ ▪

_____ ▪

NOTES

_____

_____

_____

THIS WEEK'S

DATES

PRIORITIES

TO DO

- ☐ _____
- ☐ _____
- ☐ _____
- ☐ _____
- ☐ _____

- ☐ _____
- ☐ _____
- ☐ _____
- ☐ _____
- ☐ _____

MY WEEK

MONTH

WEEK

MONDAY

....
....
....
....
....

TUESDAY

....
....
....
....
....

WEDNESDAY

....
....
....
....
....

THURSDAY

....
....
....
....
....

FRIDAY

....

....

....

....

....

THIS WEEKEND

....

....

....

....

....

WEEKLY GOALS

_____ ▢

_____ ▢

_____ ▢

_____ ▢

_____ ▢

_____ ▢

_____ ▢

_____ ▢

_____ ▢

_____ ▢

NOTES

_____

_____

_____

THIS WEEK'S

DATES

PRIORITIES

TO DO

- [ ] _____
- [ ] _____
- [ ] _____
- [ ] _____
- [ ] _____

- [ ] _____
- [ ] _____
- [ ] _____
- [ ] _____
- [ ] _____

MY WEEK

MONTH

WEEK

MONDAY

....
....
....
....
....

TUESDAY

....
....
....
....
....

WEDNESDAY

....
....
....
....
....

THURSDAY

....
....
....
....
....

FRIDAY

....

....

....

....

....

THIS WEEKEND

....

....

....

....

....

WEEKLY GOALS

_____ ▢

_____ ▢

_____ ▢

_____ ▢

_____ ▢

_____ ▢

_____ ▢

_____ ▢

_____ ▢

_____ ▢

NOTES

_____

_____

_____

THIS WEEK'S

DATES

PRIORITIES

TO DO

- [ ] _____
- [ ] _____
- [ ] _____
- [ ] _____
- [ ] _____

- [ ] _____
- [ ] _____
- [ ] _____
- [ ] _____
- [ ] _____

MY WEEK

MONTH

WEEK

MONDAY

....

....

....

....

....

TUESDAY

....

....

....

....

WEDNESDAY

....

....

....

....

....

THURSDAY

....

....

....

....

....

FRIDAY

....

....

....

....

....

THIS WEEKEND

....

....

....

....

....

WEEKLY GOALS

_____ ▪

_____ ▪

_____ ▪

_____ ▪

_____ ▪

_____ ▪

_____ ▪

_____ ▪

_____ ▪

_____ ▪

NOTES

_____

_____

_____

THIS WEEK'S

DATES

PRIORITIES

TO DO

- ☐ _____
- ☐ _____
- ☐ _____
- ☐ _____
- ☐ _____

- ☐ _____
- ☐ _____
- ☐ _____
- ☐ _____
- ☐ _____